W9-DBU-349

# BIGGEST, BADDEST BOOK OF
# MONSTERS

ANDERS HANSON & ELISSA MANN

**Consulting Editor, Diane Craig, M.A./Reading Specialist**

A Division of ABDO
**ABDO**
Publishing Company

visit us at www.abdopublishing.com

Published by ABDO Publishing Company, a division of ABDO, P.O. Box 398166, Minneapolis, Minnesota 55439.

Printed in the United States of America, North Mankato, Minnesota
062012
092012

 PRINTED ON RECYCLED PAPER

Editor: Liz Salzmann
Content Developer: Nancy Tuminelly
Cover and Interior Design and Production: Anders Hanson, Mighty Media, Inc.
Illustration Credits: Shutterstock

Library of Congress Cataloging-in-Publication Data
Hanson, Anders, 1980-
  Biggest, baddest book of monsters / Anders Hanson and Elissa Mann.
    p. cm. --  (Biggest, baddest books for boys)
  ISBN 978-1-61783-407-3 (alk. paper)
  1.  Monsters--Juvenile literature.  I. Mann, Elissa, 1990- II. Title.
  GR825.H265 2013
  398.24'54--dc23

                    2011050919

Super SandCastle™ books are created by a team of professional educators, reading specialists, and content developers around five essential components—phonemic awareness, phonics, vocabulary, text comprehension, and fluency—to assist young readers as they develop reading skills and strategies and increase their general knowledge. All books are written, reviewed, and leveled for guided reading, early reading intervention, and Accelerated Reader® programs for use in shared, guided, and independent reading and writing activities to support a balanced approach to literacy instruction.

# CONTENTS

# MONSTERS!

Monsters are fearsome creatures! But don't be afraid! Monsters aren't real!

A Chimera is part lion, part goat, and part snake.

## MONSTERS IN MYTHS

Myths are stories. There are a lot of monsters in myths. They stand for things that are wrong or evil. In many myths, a monster must be killed. This makes the world safe again.

## CRYPTIDS

Sometimes many people claim they saw an animal, but there is no proof that it exists. We call those animals cryptids. Some cryptids turn out to be real. But most are fake.

**THE GIANT SQUID**

The giant squid was once a cryptid. There was no proof that it existed until 1861.

5

# Dragons

Dragons are huge winged lizards that breathe fire. They are covered in scales. Dragons bring terror wherever they go!

# TROLLS

Trolls are huge, ugly beasts! They're super strong. But they are slow. If sunlight hits them, they turn into stone!

# GOBLINS

Goblins are small. They have pointy ears and long noses. Goblins love to play tricks on humans.

7

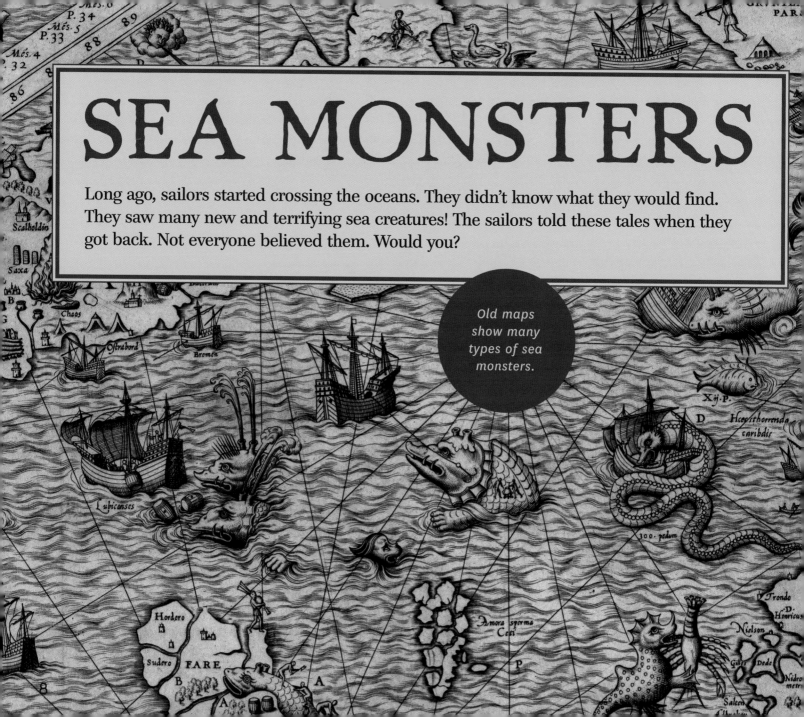

# SEA MONSTERS

Long ago, sailors started crossing the oceans. They didn't know what they would find. They saw many new and terrifying sea creatures! The sailors told these tales when they got back. Not everyone believed them. Would you?

Old maps show many types of sea monsters.

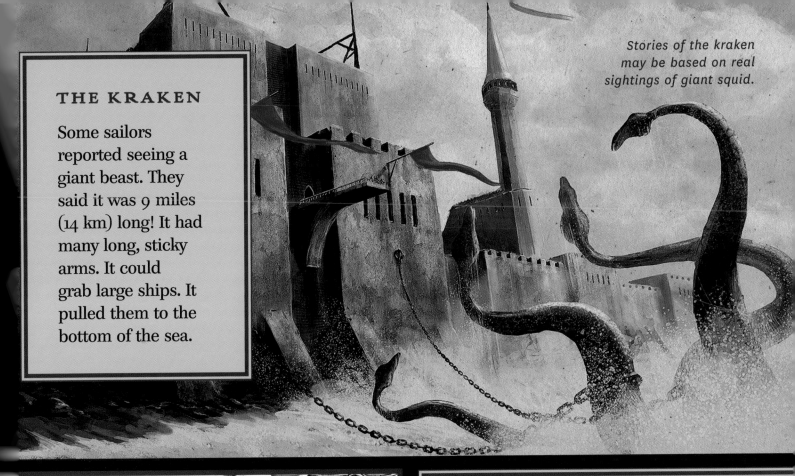

## THE KRAKEN

Some sailors reported seeing a giant beast. They said it was 9 miles (14 km) long! It had many long, sticky arms. It could grab large ships. It pulled them to the bottom of the sea.

*Stories of the kraken may be based on real sightings of giant squid.*

## THE ASP-TURTLE

Imagine stepping off a boat onto an island. Suddenly the whole island starts to move! You're not on an island at all! It's a giant sea monster! Sailors called this monster the asp-turtle.

# Lake

## MONSTERS

It was 1926. More than 30 people were at Okanagan Lake. They all said they saw a huge beast in the lake. Could they have seen a real monster? Or were they all fooled by their eyes?

## PLESIOSAUR OR DRIFTWOOD?

Many claim to have seen a lake monster. Some say they saw a plesiosaur. Others don't agree. They say it was probably driftwood.

## POSSIBLE LAKE MONSTERS

### NESSIE
**LOCH NESS, SCOTLAND**

Nessie is a famous lake monster. She was first seen more than 70 years ago!

### OGOPOGO
**OKANAGAN LAKE, CANADA**

Stories about Ogopogo have been told for 200 years. Some say it has the head of a horse and the body of a snake.

### CHAMP
**LAKE CHAMPLAIN, VERMONT, USA**

More than 300 people say they have seen Champ. Some say it looks like a huge snake.

Plesiosaurs were huge reptiles that lived in the sea. Most people think they died off long ago.

11

# BIGFOOT

**H**ave you ever seen giant footprints? Watch out! A bigfoot may be nearby! Bigfoots are giant, hairy apes. People all over the world have reported seeing them.

## EYEWITNESS ACCOUNT

In 1967, two men in California heard about huge footprints in a nearby forest. They went to check them out. Suddenly they looked up and saw a bigfoot!

One of the men filmed it. The video became famous. But not everyone believes that it was really bigfoot.

## HOW TO SPOT A BIGFOOT

Bigfoot creatures ...

- *have hands and feet that are twice the size of a human's*
- *smell awful*
- *stand 6 to 10 feet (2 to 3 m) tall*
- *are covered in thick hair*
- *are shy around humans*

## BIGFOOT SIGHTINGS AROUND THE WORLD

Other names for bigfoot-like creatures:

SASQUATCH

GRASSMAN

YETI

YOWIE

MARICOXI

BATUTUT

# VAMPIRES

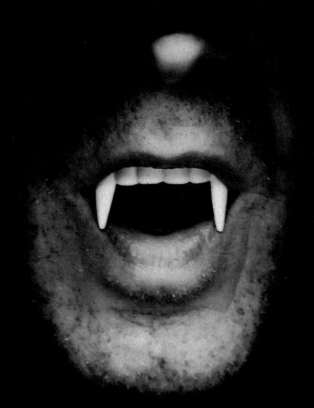

**V**ampires look like people. But they are monsters! People have told stories about them for thousands of years. All vampires have one thing in common. They drink blood.

## HOW TO SPOT A VAMPIRE

Most vampires ...

- *have pointy teeth and pale skin*
- *sleep in a **coffin***
- *are burned by sunlight*
- *hate **garlic***
- *have keen senses*

# COUNT DRACULA

The most famous vampire story is *Dracula*. It's based on a real prince. He lived in Romania 600 years ago. His name was Vlad the Impaler.

*Vlad the Impaler lived in Bran Castle. Today it is a museum.*

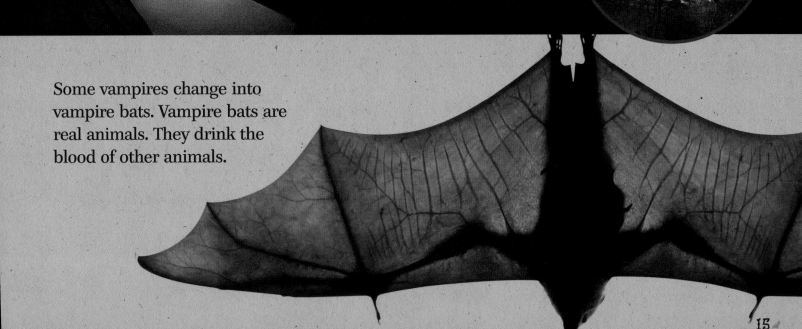

Some vampires change into vampire bats. Vampire bats are real animals. They drink the blood of other animals.

# ZOMBIES

Zombies are walking dead people. In some stories they have a terrible **disease**.

The zombie disease makes dead people come to life. Zombies try to bite people. Anyone who gets bitten becomes a zombie too!

# THE ZOMBIE APOCALYPSE

What would happen if there was a real zombie **disease**? There is no cure, so the number of zombies would keep growing.

No one would be able to stop it. Soon there would be no humans left! This is what some people call the zombie **apocalypse**.

## Mmm ... Brains

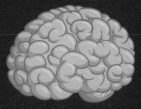

All zombies eat humans. Human brains are their favorite snack!

Ghosts don't have solid bodies. They are the spirits of dead people. But they still hang around earth. They can't hurt people. But they are kind of scary!

# GHOSTS

# America's Most Haunted Places

Angry ghosts haunt places where bad things happened. They can't leave because they are so upset! Other ghosts are friendly. They haunt places that were special to them. They stay because they don't want to leave!

## BACHELOR'S GROVE

Bachelor's Grove is an old graveyard. People say there are ghosts there. Some see a lady walking with her baby. Others see a farmer with a plow.

## ALCATRAZ

Alcatraz was a famous American prison. Today it's a museum. But many people still claim to hear the ghosts of prisoners.

## THE WHITE HOUSE

Every U.S. president except George Washington lived in the White House. Today, some visitors claim to see the ghosts of old presidents.

Werewolves change when there is a full moon.

# Werewolves

regular wolf

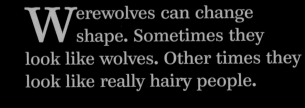

**W**erewolves can change shape. Sometimes they look like wolves. Other times they look like really hairy people.

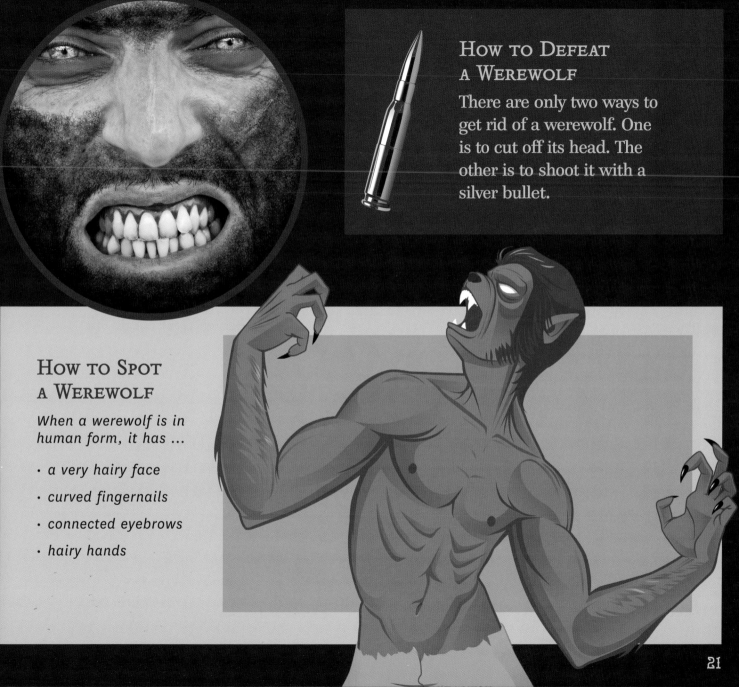

## How to Defeat a Werewolf

There are only two ways to get rid of a werewolf. One is to cut off its head. The other is to shoot it with a silver bullet.

## How to Spot a Werewolf

*When a werewolf is in human form, it has ...*

- *a very hairy face*
- *curved fingernails*
- *connected eyebrows*
- *hairy hands*

# ARE THEY REAL?

Are monsters real? Probably not. There's no proof that any of the monsters in this book exist. But some people still believe that they do.

# WHAT DO YOU KNOW ABOUT
# MONSTERS?

1. DRAGONS ARE LIZARDS THAT BREATHE FIRE.
**TRUE OR FALSE?**

2. THE KRAKEN HAD A LOT OF LONG, STICKY ARMS.
**TRUE OR FALSE?**

3. BIGFOOT IS A SMALL MONSTER.
**TRUE OR FALSE?**

4. ZOMBIES DO NOT TRY TO EAT HUMAN BRAINS.
**TRUE OR FALSE?**

ANSWERS: 1) TRUE 2) TRUE 3) FALSE 4) FALSE

# GLOSSARY

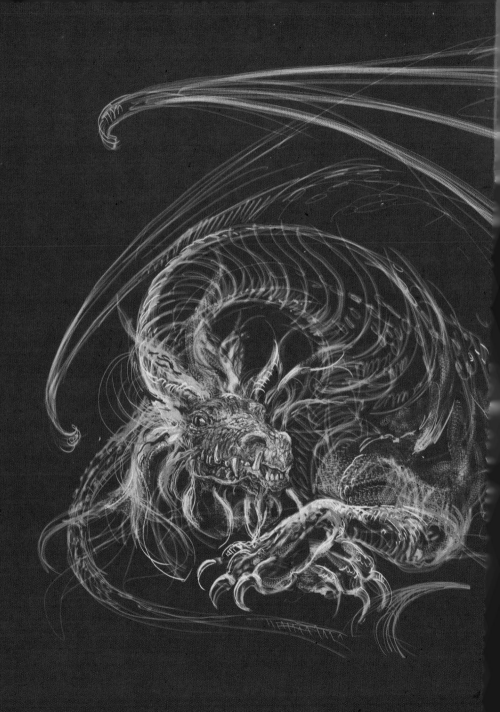

**APOCALYPSE** – a terrible disaster that affects most or all of the world.

**COFFIN** – a box a dead person is put in before being buried.

**DISEASE** – a sickness.

**GARLIC** – a plant that grows from a bulb which has a strong smell and taste and is used in cooking.